# PERSECUTION OF THE EARLY CHURCH

Medwin J. Kifita

Email- medwinkifita@gmail.com

**2020**

# CONTENT

Introduction..............................3

1. Causes of Church persecution........4

2. Church's response to persecution..8

3. How the Church Viewed Martyrs..14

4. The Edict of Milan .......................19

5. The Church in Medieval period.....26

6. The Reformation period...............30

7. Conclusion...............................34

Appendix....................................35

# INTRODUCTION

Those who have believed in the God of heaven and earth through his son Jesus Christ have continually been persecuted by rulers and kings. However, when we speak of early Christian persecution, we are referring to the time following Jesus Christ's suffering and persecution for His church. Stephen was one of the first men who suffered early Christian persecution. He was stoned to death outside the gates for the faithful manner in which he preached the Gospel. After this, a great persecution was raised against all who professed belief in Christ as the Messiah.

For more than two thousand years, God's people have borne witness to the truths of his power and lordship, the centrality of his saving work in Christ, and the hope offered freely in the gospel. Since Pentecost, God has been demonstrating this grand story of redemption in real places populated by real people, in the church.

# CHAPTER ONE
## Causes of Church persecution

Persecution of Christians in the Roman Empire occurred over a period of over two centuries between the Great Fire of Rome in 64 AD under Nero and the Edict of Milan in 313 AD, in which the Roman Emperor Constantine the Great legalized the Christian religion. This persecution of Christians in the Roman Empire was carried out by the state and also by local authorities.

Prior to Nero's accusation of arson and subsequent anti-Christian actions in 64AD, all animosity was apparently limited to intramural Jewish hostility. In Acts 18: 2-3, a Jew named Aquila and his wife Priscilla, had recently come from Italy because Emperor Claudius had ordered all the Jews to leave Rome.

Christian persecution under Nero was isolated and localized. Although it is often claimed that Christians were persecuted for their refusal to worship the emperor, general dislike for Christians likely arose from their refusal to worship the gods or take part in sacrifice, which was expected of those living in the Roman Empire.

In those days, Governors played a larger role in the actions than did Emperors, but Christians were not sought out by governors, and instead accused and prosecuted through a process termed as cognitio extra ordinem. Trials and punishments varied greatly, and sentences ranged from acquittal to death.

Apart from the fire of Rome, there were other reasons within the main areas of conflicts. To begin with, the exclusive sovereignty of Christ clashed with Caesar's claims to his own exclusive sovereignty. The Roman Empire practiced religious syncretism and did not demand loyalty to one god, but they did demand preeminent loyalty to the state, and this was expected to be demonstrated through the practices of the state religion with numerous feast and festival days throughout the year.

Persecution was heavy towards the end of Domitian's reign (89AD-96AD). The Book of Revelation, which mentions at least one instance of martyrdom (Revelation2: 13), is thought by many scholars to have been written during Domitian's reign. The nature of Christian monotheism prevented Christians from participating in anything involving 'other gods'. Christians did not participate in feast days or processionals or offer sacrifices or light incense to the gods; this produced hostility because they refused to offer incense to the Roman emperor.

Many people viewed the emperor as a god and were the embodiment of the Roman Empire, so Christians were seen as disloyal to both the empire and the state. Christianity was going to be allowed in Rome as a religion only if it could contribute to the stability of the state, and could bring no rival for the allegiance of its subjects. But in Christian monotheism, the state was not the highest good.

The fate of the Apostles and close disciples followed in succession. James the Great, the elder brother of John the Apostle, was beheaded in A.D. 44. Philip, who served in Upper Asia was scourged in Phrygia, thrown into prison and later crucified in A.D. 54.

Matthew the tax collector served the Lord in Parthia and Ethiopia where he was slain with a halberd (a shafted weapon with an axe-like cutting blade and a speared end) in the city of Nadabah, in A.D. 60.

James the brother of the Lord, served the church in Jerusalem and wrote the book of James. He suffered martyrdom at the age of ninety-four by being beaten and stoned by the Jews. Matthias, the man who was chosen to replace Judas as an apostle, was stoned at Jerusalem and then beheaded.

Andrew, the brother of Peter, preached the gospel to many Asiatic nations and was crucified on a cross at Edessa. The ends of his cross were fixed transversely in the ground, thus the derivation of the term, St. Andrew's cross.

Mark was converted to Christianity by Peter and served as amanuensis (he wrote for Peter). He was dragged to pieces by the people of Alexandria. Peter, the apostle, was sought by Nero to be put to death. Jerome wrote that Peter was crucified with his head down and his feet up, because he thought himself unworthy to be crucified in the same form and manner as the Lord.

Paul was really persecuted several times. He was scourged, stoned, and finally, Nero had him beheaded by a sword. Jude, the brother of James, commonly called Thaddeus, was crucified at Edessa in A.D. 72.

Bartholomew preached in several countries and translated the Gospel of Matthew into the language of India. He was cruelly beaten and then crucified. Thomas preached the Gospel in Parthia and India. He excited the rage of the pagan priests and was martyred by being thrust through with a spear.

Luke the author of Luke and Acts travelled with Paul through various countries and was suppose to have been hanged on olive tree by the idolatrous priests of

Greece. Simon the Zealot preached the Gospel in Mauritania, Africa, and even Britain where he was crucified in A.D. 74.

John, the Apostle whom Jesus loved, was sent from Ephesus to Rome where he was put into a cauldron of boiling oil. He escaped by a miracle, without injury, but was then banished to the Island of Patmos and there he wrote the book of Revelation. Nerva, Domitian's successor, said he was the only apostle who escaped a violent death.

After the death of all the apostles and other disciples, persecution continued to everyone who believed in the gospel. Between 109 and 111 AD, Pliny the Younger was sent by the emperor Trajan to the province of Bithynia as governor, and their conversation is considered to be a valuable historical source.

In one of his letters, Pliny reported on his actions with regard to some people who had been denounced as Christians. The letter states that, those who persisted in confessing that they were Christians he had executed or, if Roman citizens, he sent them to Rome; those who denied that they were Christians he subjected to them to the test of invoking the gods, offering them incense and a libation in the presence of an image of the emperor, and cursing Christ.

Some who admitted that they had formerly been Christians and proved, by passing the test that they were no longer Christians, he declared that Christians did not commit the crimes attributed to them. A declaration confirmed under torture by two slave women who were called deaconesses.

Pliny therefore asked the emperor whether ceasing to be a Christian was enough to secure pardon for having been one, and whether punishment was merited just for being a Christian (the name itself) or only for the crimes associated with the name.

Trajan responded that the problem could only be dealt with case by case. The authorities were not to seek Christians out, but people who were denounced and found guilty were to be punished unless, by worshiping the Roman gods, they proved they were not Christians (having denied Christ) and so obtained pardon.

We have seen that the first mass persecution occurred under Nero in A.D. 67. He was the sixth emperor of Rome and is remembered as the one who set Rome aflame and then blamed the Christians for the deaths and destruction caused by the fire. He had some Christians sewn up in skins of wild beasts and thrown to the dogs. Some Christians were dressed in shirts made stiff with wax, fixed to axletrees, and set on fire in his gardens, in order to illuminate them.

Rather than diminished the spirit of Christianity, this persecution increased the devotion and commitment of Christianity.

# CHAPTER TWO

## Church's response to persecution

Christians moved their activities from the streets to the more secluded domains of houses, shops and women's apartments, severing the normal ties between religion, tradition and public institutions like cities and nations. This privatizing of religion was another primary factor in persecution. Christians sometimes met at night in secret, and this aroused suspicion among the pagan population accustomed to religion as a public event.

By embracing the faith of the Gospel the Christians incurred the supposed guilt of an unnatural and unpardonable offence. In 250 AD, the emperor Decius issued a decree requiring public sacrifice, a formality equivalent to a testimonial of allegiance to the emperor and the established order. Although there is no evidence that the decree was intended to target Christians, it was intended as a form of loyalty oath.

Decius authorized roving commission visiting the cities and villages to supervise the execution of the sacrifices and to deliver written certificates to all citizens who performed them. Christians were often given opportunities to avoid further punishment by publicly offering sacrifices or burning incense to Roman gods, and were accused by the Romans of impiety when they refused. Refusal was punished by arrest, imprisonment, torture, and executions. Christians fled to safe havens in the countryside and some purchased their certificates, called libelli.

The persecutions culminated with Diocletian and Galerius at the end of the third and beginning of the 4th century. Their anti-Christian actions, considered the largest, were to be the last major Roman pagan action. The Edict of Serdica, also called Edict of Toleration by Galerius, was issued in 311 in Serdica (today Sofia, Bulgaria) by the Roman emperor Galerius, officially ending the Diocletianic persecution of Christianity in the East.

Later on, Constantine the Great came into power and in 313 completely legalized Christianity (Discussed in chapter 3). When Constantine became emperor in

306AD, he based the empire in a new city on the site of an ancient Greek colony named Byzantium. He then renamed the city Constantinople in his honor and became the capital of a huge empire. The city is today called Istanbul in Turkey.

These persecutions heavily influenced the development of Christianity, shaping Christian theology and the structure of the Church. The effects of the persecutions included the writing of explanations and defenses of the Christian religion.

As it is Doctor Luke put it in Acts, "they continued steadfastly in the apostles' doctrine". They relied on the apostles to communicate to them who Jesus was and what He had done. They just trusted in Jesus; now they wanted to know more.

It was a learning Church; it persisted in listening to the apostles as they taught. One of the great dangers of the Church is to look back instead of forward. Because the riches of Christ are inexhaustible, we should always be going forward. We should count it a wasted day when we do not learn something new and when we have not penetrated more deeply into the wisdom and the grace of God.

They continued in steadfastly in fellowship: The ancient Greek word koinonia (translated here as fellowship) has the idea of association, communion, fellowship, and participation; it means to share in something. The Christian life is meant to be full of fellowship, of sharing one with another.

They continued in steadfastly in the breaking of bread: Even living so close to the time when Jesus was crucified, they still never wanted to forget what He did on the cross. How much more important is it for us to never forget?

Communion is vital to the health of the church corporately and to believers individually. Paul wrote to the church at Corinth that, because they took Communion lightly, many of them were weak, sick, and even dying unnecessarily (1 Corinthians 11:30). Whenever we fail to give worth to the Lord's Table, I believe we jeopardize not only our spiritual life, but our physical, marital, and emotional life as well.

They continued in steadfastly in prayers. Whenever God's work is done, God's people gather for prayer and worship. They devoted themselves to the breaking of bread and to the prayers. Obviously, that is a reference to something formal – to worship in which the people got together and praised God.

It was a praying Church; these early Christians knew that they could not meet life in their own strength and that they did not need to. They always went in to

God before they went out to the world; they were able to meet the problems of life because they had met Christ first.

The apostles' doctrine and fellowship, in the breaking of bread, and in prayers: Everything else we read about the power and glory of the early church flows from this foundation of the word, fellowship, remembrance of Jesus' work on the cross, and prayer.

These were the four institutions of the early church. First of all, the apostles' doctrine: the study of the Word of God. Second, the fellowship: the koinonia-a very interesting Greek word. Its implications are beyond translation into English. But it is coming together, interrelating, becoming a part of each other, a strong bond and tie and communion and commonness and fellowship. Breaking of bread is the symbol of that inner relationship and prayers.

Many of the things that the church does today are not listed here. I think a lot of the things that the church does today are extraneous and supercilious, and we would do well to let them die a natural death instead of trying to keep them alive by artificial means.

Then fear came upon every soul: This was evidence of the power of God. (Acts 2:43) It was a reverent Church; in verse 43, the word which translates as fear has the idea of awe in it. It was said of a great Greek that he moved through this world as if it were a temple. Many signs and wonders were done: This was evidence of the power of God. Where God is at work, lives will be touched in miraculous ways.

If we expect great things from God and attempt great things for God, things happen. More things would happen if we believed that God and we together could make them happen

Now all who believed were together, and had all things in common: With the influx of more than 3,000 believers, most of whom stayed in Jerusalem and didn't have jobs, the family of Christians had to share if they were to survive.

The early believers were not Communists. They were "commonists." And there's a big difference. Communism says: What's yours is mine. "Commonism" says: What's mine is yours. The believers in Jerusalem pooled whatever resources they had for the express purpose of allowing the new believers to remain in Jerusalem rather than having to return to the lands from which they came from.

Communism is a description of a political and economic system of such a different character that it is anachronistic and misleading to use the term in the present context.

We shouldn't regard this as an early experiment in communism because it was voluntary, temporary, and flawed to the extent that the church in Jerusalem was in continual need of financial support from other churches. Also, we don't have any evidence this continued very long.

All who believed were together: The Jews had a tremendous custom of hospitality during any major feast like Pentecost. Visitors were received into private homes, and no one could charge for giving a bed or a room to a visitor or for supplying their basic needs. The Christians took this tremendous feast-time hospitality and made it an everyday thing.

Sold their possessions and their goods, and divided them among all, as anyone had need: The power of God is evident here because Jesus became much more important to them than their possessions. These early Christians had an intense feeling of responsibility for each other. Real Christians cannot bear to have too much when others have too little.

It was a worshipping Church (verse 46); they never forgot to visit God's house. We must remember that 'God knows nothing of solitary religion.' Things can happen when we come together. God's Spirit moves upon his worshipping people.

Christians met together for their own religious gatherings. They met in one another's homes and broke bread together in a spirit of intense and sincere joy. The idea is that they held common meals which included the breaking of bread; we may compare Paul's description of the common church meal at Corinth, which included the celebration of the Lord's Supper (1 Cori. 11: 17-34).

The joy that characterizes these gatherings was no doubt inspired by the Spirit and may have been associated with the conviction that the Lord Jesus was present with them.

Their Christian experience was daily, joyful and simple. This was the reason why the early Church grew so fast. "And the Lord added to the church daily those who were being saved". This is God's prescription for church growth. If we take care to follow the example of Acts 2: 42-47, God will take care of growing the church Himself.

As the Christians were seen and heard by the other people in Jerusalem, their activities formed an opportunity for witness. Once again Luke refers to the process of becoming a Christian as being saved.

One writer said, "Today the church is spending all of its efforts in church growth programs. How to increase our attendance? Studying psychology and sociology and making demographic studies of communities and determining how to appeal to the people of this particular community, what type of an advertising program will be most effective, taking polls and census and putting everything together so that we can have a church growth program because we want to add so many members to our church."

You can get professionals to come in and do all of these studies and, for a fee, they will go ahead and develop your whole program. There are other professionals who will come in and set up a whole financial program for us, and they will, for ten percent of the take, will set up the whole program of how to take you. And many churches hire these professionals for the church growth, or the fundraising programs. The early church didn't know anything of that. They were not very sophisticated, and they hadn't gone to seminary.

So all they could do is what they knew to do, just get together and study the Word and pray and fellowship, break bread. "And the Lord added daily to the church those who were being saved." It was a natural spontaneous growth as the Lord added to the church.

But God has not changed. For sure God's hand is not short that He can't save, neither is His ear heavy. But the problem is that, we are no longer relying upon God; we are no longer relying upon the Holy Spirit. We have put men's devices and man's ways. And we have forsaken the Word of God and gone to entertaining programs.

# CHAPTER THREE

## HOW THE EARLY CHURCH VIEWED MARTYRS

The word martyr means "witness" and is used as such throughout the New Testament. However, as the Roman Empire became increasingly hostile toward Christianity, the distinctions between witnessing and suffering became blurred and finally nonexistent. In the second century, **martyr** became a technical term for a person who had died for Christ, while **confessor** was defined as one who proclaimed

Christ's lordship at trial but did not suffer the death penalty.

A passage from Eusebius describes the survivors of the persecution in Lyons (177 AD in what is today France). "They were also so zealous in their imitation of Christ that, though they had attained honour, and had borne witness, not once or twice, but many times, yet they did not proclaim themselves martyrs, nor did they suffer us to address them by this name.

If any one of us, in letter or conversation, spoke of them as martyrs, they rebuked him sharply, and they reminded us of the martyrs, who had already departed, and said, 'They are already martyrs whom Christ has deemed worthy to be taken up in their confession, having sealed their testimony by their departure; but we are lowly and humble confessors.'"

The ideal of martyrdom did not originate with the Christian Church; it was inspired by the passive resistance of pious Jews during the Maccabean revolt (173—164 B.C.). Antiochus IV, the tyrannical Seleucid king, ignited the revolution by a variety of barbarous acts, including banning Palestinian Jews from religious practices such as circumcision.

The Maccabean period gave stories of avenging rebels such as Judas Maccabeus. What prompted Christians to emulate the passive resisters such as Eleazar, rather than armed revolutionaries like Judas Maccabeus?

To answer this question one needs to look no further than to Jesus himself. The church understood martyrdom as an imitation of Christ. The Lord was the example of non-violence at his own trial and execution, declaring that his servants would not fight because his kingdom was not of this world.

Jesus' words burned themselves deeply into the collective psyche of the Ante-Nicene church: "If someone strikes you on one cheek, turn to him the other also (Luke 6:29); do not resist an evil person (Matt. 5:39); blessed are those who are persecuted because of righteousness (Matt. 5:10); if they persecuted me, they will persecute you also (John 15:20)."

Paul and the other New Testament authors sustained and developed the theme that followers of Christ were to suffer for their Lord. A believer's weapons were not composed of iron or bronze but were made of spirit (Eph. 6:13).

Stephen, the first Christian martyr, died a Christ-like death, praying earnestly for his tormentors. Eusebius, the church historian, called Stephen "the perfect martyr", thus he became a prototype for all martyrs to follow.

The martyr's non-violent response to trial and torture was never equated with resignation. For the early church, the act of martyrdom was a spiritual battle of epic proportion against the powers of hell itself. Justin, for example, wrote an apologetic to Emperor Antoninus Pius, charging that his punishment of Christians without examination was "by the instigation of demons."

Perpetua recorded in her prison diary prior to her death that she had a vision in which she defeated an Egyptian wrestler before Christ, the heavenly umpire. Conquering this symbol of the Evil One, she was awarded apples, the prize in Apollo's games at Carthage.

Another martyr, Blandina, was described as "the small, the weak and the despised, who had put on Christ the great and invincible Champion, and who in many rounds vanquished the adversary and through conflict was crowned with the crown of incorruptibility."

For early Christians, such a battle was not waged alone. The church (as G. W. Lampe notes), understood the believer's suffering and death as a concrete and literal realization of death and burial with Christ, enacted figuratively in every convert's baptism (Rom. 6:3).

Ignatius of Antioch, on his way to martyrdom at Rome, wrote to the church not to take action to prevent his death, for he wished to attain to Christ and to be an imitator of the passion of Christ his God.

The New Testament afforded to the early church numerous explications of this theme;

To persecute Christians is to persecute Jesus himself (Acts 9:5),

Christ's disciples would suffer as he did Christ himself (John 15:20), Believers are to be crucified with Christ (Gal. 2:20),

Christians are to rejoice in so far as you share Christ's sufferings that you may rejoice and be glad when his glory is revealed (1 Pet. 4:13).

Martyrs not only represented Christ, but also found Christ actually present with them, in a mystical way, during their torment. At the death of Blandina in Lyons in177AD, it was said "they saw him who was crucified on their behalf in the person of their sister."

The church understood the source of the martyr's strength and testimony to be the Holy Spirit. Only by his inspiration could such powerful proclamation be given before hostile authorities. The martyrs relied on Jesus' promise; "Whenever you are arrested and brought to trial, do not worry beforehand about what to say. Just say whatever is given you at the time, for it is not you speaking, but the Holy Spirit" (Mark. 13:11).

Those who confessed their faith in the face of persecution were seen as receiving a word of revelation and proclamation much like the Old Testament prophets. Vettius, spokesman for the martyrs of Lyons, was described as having "in himself the Spirit of Zechariah," (who was identified in Luke 1:67).

The Spirit fell on slave and free, baptized and unbaptized, granting dreams and visions as he saw fit. For example, Polycarp (the bishop of Smyrna martyred AD155) saw his pillow on fire, understanding the vision as a prophecy regarding the kind of death he would die. Basileides, an Alexandrian soldier, was granted a vision of the martyred Potamiaena, who informed him that he would soon have the privilege of dying for Christ. In both instances the prophetic visions were fulfilled.

The negative side to the assurance of inspiration during trial and torture was the danger of apostasy under the same conditions. The Shepherd of Hermas declared that a servant who denies the Lord is evil.

Cyprian went further; reminding the mistakes that apostasy is equivalent to blasphemy of the Holy Spirit. Jesus Christ said, 'whoever shall confess me before men, him will I also confess before my Father who is in heaven, but whosoever shall deny me, him will I deny.'

Because they stood against apostasy, and because they possessed gifts of prophecy and visions, martyrs and confessors were held in high regard in the church. Their spiritual authority, in fact, rivalled that of bishops. In one instance, Saturus of Carthage saw a vision in which he and Perpetua, (both martyrs to be) were called upon to mediate a dispute between a bishop and his elders.

The early church also believed in martyrs as master intercessors. The First Epistle of John alludes to the power of intercession: "If anyone sees his brother commit a sin that does not lead to death, he should pray and God will give him life" (1 John 5:16). Numerous stories were circulated of almost legendary feats of prayer performed by martyrs during their lifetimes. Thus it was not difficult for Christians at that time to imagine these same prayer warriors interceding at the heavenly court after death.

While Christ's death remained central to the early church's understanding of salvation, it was believed that a martyr's death effaced all sins committed after baptism. Melito of Sardis claimed, "There are two things which give remission of sins; baptism and suffering for the sake of Christ." Tertullian echoed this, writing to martyrs: "Your blood is the key to Paradise."

The belief in the virtue of martyrdom generated the phenomenon of "volunteering," whereby numbers of Christians actively sought persecution and death. In one account, a Roman governor was interrupted in his courtroom by a Christian named Euplus who shouted, "I am a Christian. I want to die." His request was granted.

The sentiment of the early church towards its martyrs moved from love to reverence to veneration. The author of the 'account of the martyrdom of Polycarp' wrote: "For him as Son of God we adore; the martyrs, as disciples and imitators of the Lord, we reverence as they deserve on account of their unsurpassable loyalty to their King and Teacher." Martyrs were honoured by having their heavenly birthdays celebrated annually.

The celebration service was held at the grave of the deceased with prayer, oblations, Communion, and a reading of the martyr's history of suffering and death. This practice was quite contrary to Christianity's Jewish roots, for Judaism, following the Mosaic law, held that a grave was unclean. Thus a third-century

Syrian Christian advised fellow believers to meet in their cemeteries without fear of impurity.

It is not certain exactly when the honour paid to the martyred dead was transferred to their physical remains, but the account of the martyrdom of Polycarp, written in the second century, includes a statement that the church of Smyrna counted the bones of the saint "more valuable than precious stones and finer than gold." Believers in Antioch held the remains of Ignatius in high esteem, while Cyprian's blood and clothing became objects of veneration.

The emphasis on procuring martyrs' relics produced many abuses but did not dampen the church's desire to honour its faithful dead. The importance of relics grew to such proportion that the Seventh Ecumenical Council (in Nicea in 787) decreed that relics must be placed in the altar of a new church before it could be consecrated.

Any abuses surrounding the honouring of the martyrs should not blind us to the spiritual debt the whole church owes to these brave souls. By their faithfulness to Christ in spite of torture and death, these men, women, and children proclaimed to the world that Jesus, and not Caesar, is Lord. In the words of the Book of Revelation, "They overcame him by the blood of the Lamb and by the word of their testimony; they did not love their lives so much as to shrink from death (Rev12:11)."

# CHAPTER FOUR

## THE EDICT OF MILAN

During the winter months of the year 313 AD, Emperor Constantine of the Roman Empire met in Milan with his rival emperor, Licinius, to reconsider the policies regarding the Christian population. Their agreement would be known by most as the Edict of Milan; a continuation to the already existing Edict of Toleration declared by Galerius, the third living Roman Emperor, just two years prior.

The main intentions behind the edict were to abolish practices that persecuted the Christians and to begin accepting their religion in Rome, "no man whatever should be refused complete toleration, who has given up his mind either to the cult of the Christians or to the religion which he personally feels best suited to himself." The edict also declared the abolishment of "all conditions whatever which are embodied in former orders directed to you the governors of the Roman provinces, offices about the Christians" and that "the places at which they were used formerly to assemble be restored to the Christians."

Throughout the course of the next century, the Christian religion would transition from being persecuted to being the official religion of the Roman Empire. As a result, some scholars argue that the Edict of Milan began the rise of the Christian religion because the edict preceded the legitimization of Christianity in the Roman Empire. However, this is not the case. The Edict of Milan did not cause the spread of the Christian religion, but rather, it was a response to an already growing movement.

The most credible source of the Edict of Milan comes from the writings of Lactantius, a Christian apologist who lived during the years 250-325 AD. Lucius Lactantius et al., "The Edict of Milan" In A New Eusebius: Documents Illustrating the History of the Church to AD 337, states that, roughly, 50 years before the time of Constantine and Licinius, Emperor Diocletian, the predecessor to Constantine, despised the Christians.

One of the reasons why Diocletian persecuted Christians was that, he wanted to restore Rome to the way Emperor Augustus ruled it with the traditional Pagan gods at the forefront of religion.

Augustus' empire was so large that it stretched from Spain all the way to Egypt, but Diocletian recognized that he alone could not control it.

He split the land into the west and east half to deal with the growing problems like the increase of barbarian invasions, and he accepted a man named Valerius as his co-emperor to lead the western half of Rome. Diocletian himself would rule the east. Despite this, if he wanted to be recognized like Augustus, he needed to be enveloped in divinity, or at least convince the people of that. Augustus himself was viewed as a god sent from the heavens, and thus Diocletian had to be a god too. However, the Christians living in the Roman Empire stood in the way of this because they did not believe in any other gods besides their one God, and they especially did not believe that mankind could be divine.

Because the Christians did not view Diocletian as divine, he could then justify using them as a scapegoat for everything undesirable happening to Rome; disease attacks, barbarian invasions, and general social disruptions. To Diocletian, the Pagan gods were unhappy with Rome because the Christians were allowed to practice their religion. Diocletian used any excuse he could to burn their churches, stone them in the streets, and essentially persecute them into submission of his divine status.

Most persecutions were declared in the form of edicts, some of which Eusebius of Caesarea, one of the first Christian historians, elaborates on. In his words, "an imperial letter was everywhere promulgated, ordering the razing of the churches to the ground the destruction by fire of the Scriptures, and proclaiming that those who held high positions would lose all civil rights, while those in households, if they persisted in their profession of Christianity, would be deprived of their liberty."

To humiliate the Christians even further, Eusebius adds on in another edict that was under Diocletian's rule, "all the people in a body should sacrifice and offer libations to idols." This edict forced Christians to go against the very fundamental belief that there is only one God, but Diocletian needed to impose this in order to maintain authority and be seen as divine. All the people had to submit to the emperor in order for the nation to be united. Emperor Diocletian, however, was not divine; he was a human being doomed to eventually die.

In the year 305 AD, he stepped down from the throne after becoming too sick to lead. He convinced Valerius to do the same and eventually died in 311 AD.

The two thrones then went on to the next emperors in line; Galerius in eastern Rome, and Constantius in western Rome. But, the transition into new leadership did not come peacefully. For the next few years, those in any relation to previous emperorship struggled for the power of the throne. This continued until only three candidates remained: Galerius' friend Licinius, Valerius' son Maxentius, and Constantius' son Constantine.

The three would war with each other in order to eliminate the other candidates and guarantee the throne. In one historic battle between Constantine and Maxentius on the Milvian Bridge in 312 AD, Constantine's men slaughtered Maxentius' until they pushed his forces to retreat back to Rome. Maxentius himself did not survive as he drowned in a river before reaching the city.

Baker Academic (2013), Divine intervention also played a factor in the battle. Eusebius explains that, the night before the battle, Constantine saw with his own eyes the trophy of a cross of light in the heavens, above the sun, and bearing the inscription, "Conquer by this sign". In his sleep the Son of God appeared to him with the same sign which he had seen in the heavens." The next morning, Constantine instructed his men to replace the original symbols on their shields and banners with the symbol of Christ.

If Constantine really was spoken to by the Christian God, then this battle most likely contributed to Constantine's future acceptance of Christianity.

Afterwards, there were only two emperors left: Constantine and Licinius. Instead of pursuing war, the two declared a truce and met to begin developing the Edict of Milan. Some of the lines in the Edict of Milan, however, suggest that the rise of Christianity already started and that the edict was not what began it. For example, one section states that "the places at which they formerly used to assemble, be restored to the Christians."

Lactantius used the words formerly restored because Christian's property was to be restored as if they had already established themselves in Rome. The Edict of Milan did not call for the establishment of Christian property but instead its reestablishment.

Baker Academic (2013) noted that, Constantine had to be generous to them. At that time, Constantine was not even a declared Christian; he was still a Pagan. Yet that did not stop him from promoting the Christianization of the empire. Constantine personally gave grants to build churches and he allowed Christians to be government officials when this had not been allowed to before.

Roughly a year after the Edict of Milan was established, Licinius began attacking Christians and destroying their churches. Yet Constantine still defended them. He gathered his army and led an invasion into Licinius' territory until he had him hanged. With this in mind, some historians argue that the Edict of Milan marked a significant shift in population favouring the Christians.

Theological historian, David Knowles, explains this in his paper regarding the Christian church as a political entity: "with the conversion of Constantine, there took place the most radical change that has ever occurred in Christendom . . . the church became a state church with the head of the state as its protector." When Christianity became adopted as the official religion, the Roman Empire would never be the same.

However, there are other factors that have led to the rise of Christianity, and one formal declaration of the large presence of Christianity is not the only factor. New Testament scholar, Helmut Koester, points out in his book, History and Literature of Early Christianity, that the Apostle Paul played a huge role in spreading Christianity. Koester states, "Although Paul's missionary effort constituted but a small segment of the beginnings of Christianity, it became very important and had momentous consequences."

This was a message that would begin spreading long before the Edict of Milan. The Christian lifestyle that Paul advocates involves charity and giving back to those that have less. Living with this moral conduct encouraged kindness among people. This also meant treating each other equally regardless of gender, race, or ethnicity because all are equal in the eyes of God. Thus, Christianity often appealed more strongly to women.

Religion sociologist, Rodney Stark, analyzes the differences between women's and men's support of Christianity during the religion's early roots. Christianity regarded women far differently than Paganism. Where Paganism discouraged giving birth to girls or children with irregularities, Christianity prohibited abortion and infanticide practices. A woman could love her child regardless of sex or ability.

Pagan families also forbade women from receiving an education, forced them to marry at puberty, and required them to live under the domination of their husband.

Meanwhile, Christian women were under less drastic circumstances. Christian women were not pressured remarry if widowed — unlike the Pagan women. Christian women could, and often did, marry at an older age and had more choice in who they married. Christianity also encouraged women to remain chaste until marriage equally as much as men. In all these ways, Stark states, "the Christian women enjoyed far greater a marital security and equality than did her Pagan neighbour."

The promise of independence and the ability to make their own decisions without a man dictating them made Christianity an appealing religious lifestyle for women. The Christian religion also helped spread hope when Paganism often failed in this aspect.

During the year 250 AD when the Plague of Cyprian struck Rome, mass deaths were common in Roman population. The spread of the disease is still unknown to medical historians.

It is proposed that the epidemic could have been smallpox or measles. Regardless, this left the Roman Empire prone to attacks from neighbouring states, such as the Gaul and Germanic tribes. Ironically, even though emperors, like Diocletian himself, blamed the Christians for these events, Christianity as a whole strongly benefited from the plague and the invasions.

Where Pagan gods failed to protect their followers, Christianity offered peace of mind by explaining that there is a purpose in everything and a prosperous future awaiting those who have faith in the Christian God. Because there were far fewer Christians compared to Romans, the population of Christians would remain a small percentage while the Roman population percentage would decrease dramatically.

According to Rodney Stark, this meant that "large numbers of people, especially Pagans, would have lost the bounds that once might have restrained them from becoming Christians." As a result, there existed less societal pressure to be a Pagan and fewer constraints seeking hope from Christianity. The hope Christianity created offered a compelling alternative to Paganism for the suffering Romans.

The Christian following was not just the men but the children as well because women are the ones who give birth and raised them. Eventually, the small group of Christians started in Jerusalem would grow to be a huge population of Romans to whom Constantine would have to respond and acknowledge.

The Christian population grew so large that the only way that Paganism could ever return was if the Christians were simply removed from the Empire or killed off. Roman history after Constantine's death in 337 AD would prove that no other methods would work when his nephew, Julian, became emperor.

Julian attempted to revert the Roman Empire back to Paganism by proposing several edicts that targeted the Christians. This would in turn diminish the Christian presence in the empire. Several of Julian's propositions modelled edicts similar to those of Diocletian most declared that, Pagan temples were to be rebuilt and that Pagan practices should be adopted again.

However, these changes did close to nothing in minimizing the strength of the Christian movement. The attempt to revive Paganism died along with Julian because the next emperor Theodosius' policies prohibited most Pagan practices. Sacrifices and visits to Pagan temples were banned and Christianity became established as the official religion of the Roman Empire.

Constantine's actions and the edict itself certainly helped Christianity become a more prevalent political entity, but the edict's effects on Christianity's growth in followers fall short in comparison to the effects that the religion itself, the travels of Paul the Apostle, and the unique circumstances surrounding Rome had.

None of these reasons are because of the Edict of Milan or Constantine's actions, but instead, they are a response to the presence of the Christians. Afterwards, Christianity would become the backbone of centuries of history and politics in the Byzantine Empire, the Medieval Kingdoms, the Renaissance era, and all the way up to the Modern age.

# CHAPTER FIVE

## THE CHURCH IN MEDIEVAL PERIOD

Religious practice in medieval Europe (476-1500 AD) was dominated by the Catholic Church. The majority of the population was Christian, and Christian at this time meant "Catholic" as there was initially no other form of that religion. The rampant corruption of the medieval Church, however, gave rise to reformers such as John Wycliffe (1330-1384 AD) and Jan Hus (1369-1415 AD) and religious sects which were condemned as heresies by the Church (such as the Bogomils and Cathars, among many others). Even so, the Church maintained its power and exercised enormous influence over people's daily lives from the king on his throne to the peasant in the field.

The Bogomils and Cathars were radical dualistic Christian sects that differed from mainstream Christianity on a number of important doctrinal issues. The Bogomils and Cathars challenged traditional medieval Christian views about marriage, sex, and the religious authority of women. Although both groups ultimately were dismissed as heretical, the alternative notions of sex and gender they purposed had an impact on the development of Christianity.

The Bogomils emerged in the late tenth century when a Bulgarian priest who took the name Bogomil, meaning "worthy of the pity of God," broke with mainstream Roman Catholicism and professed a belief in a dualistic form of Christianity. He preached about a world starkly divided between the forces of good (God) and those of evil (Satan). That interpretation of Christianity quickly spread throughout medieval Europe.

The Church regulated and defined an individual's life, literally, from birth to death and was thought to continue its hold over the person's soul in the afterlife. The Church was the manifestation of God's will and presence on earth, and its dictates were not to be questioned, even when it was apparent that many of the clergy were working far more steadily toward their own interests than those of their God.

A dramatic blow to the power of the Church came in the form of the **Black Death pandemic** of 1347-1352 during which people began to doubt the power of the clergy who could do nothing to stop people from dying or the plague from spreading. Even so, the Church repeatedly crushed dissent, silenced reformers, and massacred heretical sects until the Protestant Reformation (1517-1648 AD) which broke the Church's power and allowed for greater freedom of thought and religious expression.

The Church claimed authority from God through Jesus Christ who, according to the Bible, designated his apostle Peter as "the rock upon which my church will be built, to whom he gave the keys of the kingdom of heaven." (Matthew 16:18-19). Peter was therefore regarded as the first Pope, the head of the church, and all others as his successors endowed with the same divine authority.

By the time of the middle Ages, the Church had an established hierarchy: Pope – the head of the Church

Cardinals – advisors to the Pope administrators of the Church Bishops/Archbishops – ecclesiastical superiors over a cathedral or region Priests – ecclesiastical authorities over a parish, village, or town church

The Church maintained the belief that Jesus Christ was the only begotten son of the one true God as revealed in the Hebrew Scriptures (which would become the Christian Old Testament) and that they prophesied Christ's coming. The date of the earth and history of humanity was all revealed through the scriptures which made up the Christian Bible – considered the word of God and the oldest book in the world – which was consulted as a handbook on how to live according to divine will and gain everlasting life in heaven upon one's death.

Interpretation of the Bible, however, was too great a responsibility for the average person, and so the clergy was a spiritual necessity. In order to talk to God or understand the Bible correctly, one relied on one's priest as that priest was ordained by his superior who was, in turn, ordained by another, all under the authority of the Pope, God's representative on earth.

The Church hierarchy maintained the social hierarchy. One was born into a certain class, followed the profession of one's parents, and died as they had. Social mobility was extremely rare to nonexistent since the Church taught that it was God's will one had been born into a certain set of circumstances and attempting to improve one's lot was tantamount to claiming God had made a mistake. People, therefore, accepted their lot and made the best of it.

The lives of the people of the middle Ages revolved around the Church. People, especially women, were known to attend church three to five times daily for prayer and at least once a week for services, confession, and acts of contrition for repentance. The Church paid no taxes and was supported by the people of a town or city. Citizens were responsible for supporting the parish priest and Church overall through a tithe of ten percent of their income. Tithes paid for baptism ceremonies, confirmations, and funerals as well as saint's day festivals and holy day festivals such as Easter celebrations.

The centre of a congregation's life in a small-town church or city cathedral was not the altar but the baptismal font. This was a free-standing stone receptacle/basin used for infant or adult baptism – often quite large and deep, which also served to determine a person's guilt or innocence when one was charged with a crime.

To clear one's name, a person would submit to an ordeal in which one was bound and dropped into the font. If the accused floated, it was a clear indication of guilt; if the accused sank, it meant innocence but the accused would often drown.

Under the reign of the English king Athelstan (924-939 AD), the procedure for the ordeal was codified as law. If anyone pledges to undergo the ordeal, he is then to come three days before to the mass-priest whose duty was to consecrate it (the ordeal) and live off bread and water and salt and vegetables, and be present at mass on each of those three days, and make his offering and go to communion on the day on which he shall go to the ordeal, and swear then the oath that he is guiltless of that charge according to the common law, before he goes to the ordeal. (Brooke, 107)

There was also the ordeal of iron in which the accused was forced to hold or carry a hot poker. If the person could hold the red-hot iron without burning and blistering their hands, they were innocent; there are no records of anyone being found innocent. The ordeal of water was also carried out by streams, rivers, and lakes. Women accused of witchcraft, for example, were often tied in a sack and thrown into a body of water.

If they managed to escape and come to the surface, they were found guilty and then executed, but they most often drowned.

Ordeals, like executions, were a form of public entertainment and, as with festivals, marriages, and other events in community life, were paid for by the people's tithe to the Church. The lower class, as usual, bore the brunt of the Church's expenses but the nobility was also required to donate large sums to the Church to ensure a place for them in heaven or to lessen their time in purgatory.

The Church's teachings on purgatory were that, it is an afterlife realm between heaven and hell where souls remained trapped until they had paid for their sins. This generated enormous wealth for various clergy who sold writs known as indulgences, promising a shorter stay in purgatory for a price.

Relics were another source of income, and it was common for unscrupulous clerics to sell fake splinters of Christ's cross, a saint's finger or toe, a vial of water from the Holy Land, or any number of objects, which would allegedly bring luck or ward off misfortune.

The teachings of the Church were a certainty to the people of the middle Ages. There was no room for doubt, and questions were not tolerated. One was either in the Church or out of it, and if out, one's interactions with the rest of the community were limited. Jews, for example, lived in their own neighbourhoods surrounded by Christians and were regularly treated quite poorly.

A citizen of Europe, therefore who did not belong to either of these faiths - had to adhere to the orthodox vision of the Church in order to interact with family, community, and make a living. If one could not do so (or at least appear to do so), the only option was a so-called heretical sect.

# CHAPTER SIX

## THE REFORMATION

The heretical sects of the middle Ages were uniformly responses to the clear corruption and greed of the Church. The immense wealth of the Church, accrued through tithes and lavish gifts, only inspired a desire for even greater wealth which translated as power. An archbishop could, and frequently did, threaten a noble, a town, or even a monastery with excommunication, by which one was exiled from the Church and so from the grace of God and commerce with fellow citizens for any reason.

Even well-known and devout religious figures such as Hildegard of Bingen (1098-1179 AD) were subject to discipline along these lines for disagreeing with an ecclesiastical superior.

The priests were notoriously corrupt and, in many cases, were illiterate parasites who only held their position due to family influence and favour. Scholar G. G. Coulton cites a letter of 1281 AD in which the writer warns how "the ignorance of the priests precipitates the people into the ditch of error".

The medieval mystic Margery Kempe (1342-1438 AD) challenged the wealthy clerics to reform their corruption while, almost 200 years before, Hildegard of Bingen had done the same as had men like John Wycliffe and Jan Hus. The Church was not interested in reform, however, because it had the last word on any subject as God's voice on earth.

Those who found the abuses of the Church too intolerable and were seeking an honest spiritual experience instead of an unending pay-to-pray scheme, which not even death could halt, joined religious sects outside the Church and attempted to live peacefully in their own communities. The best-known of these were the Cathars (discussed in chapter five) of Southern France who, while they interacted with the Catholic communities they lived near or in, had their own services, rituals, and belief system.

These kinds of communities were routinely condemned by the Church and destroyed, their members massacred, and whatever lands they had confiscated as Church property.

Even an orthodox community which adhered to Catholic teachings such as the Beguines was condemned because it begun spontaneously as a response to the needs of the people and was not initiated by the Church.

The Beguines were laywomen who lived as nuns and served their community, holding all possessions in common and living a life of poverty and service to others, but they were not approved by the Church and were therefore condemned; they were disbanded along with their male counterparts, the Beghards, in the 12th century.

These groups, and others like them, attempted to assert spiritual autonomy based on the scriptural authority of the Bible, without any of the Church's trappings or elaborate ritual.

The Cathars believed that Christ never died on the cross and was therefore never resurrected but that, instead, the son of God had been spiritually offered for the sins of humanity on a higher place. They further advocated for the feminine principle in the divine, revering a goddess of wisdom known as Sophia, to whom they devoted their lives.

Living simply and serving the surrounding community, the Cathars amassed no wealth, their priests owned nothing and were highly respected as holy men even by Catholics, and Cathar communities offered worthwhile goods and services.

The Beguines, while never claiming any beliefs outside of orthodox, were equally devout and selfless in their efforts to help the poor and, especially, poor single mothers and their children. Both of these movements, however, offered people an alternative to the Church, and the medieval Church found that intolerable. Any change in people's attitudes toward religion threatened the power of the Church, and the Church had enough power to crush such movements even in cases where sects such as the Cathars had significant support and protection.

John Wycliffe and his followers (known as Lollards) had been calling for reformation since the 14th century CE, and it might be difficult for a modern-day reader to fully understand why no serious attempts were made at reform, but this is simply because the modern era offers so many different legitimate avenues for religious expression. In the middle Ages, it was inconceivable that there could be any valid belief system other than the Church.

Heaven, hell, and purgatory were all very real places to the people of the middle Ages, and one could not risk offending God by criticizing his Church and damning one's self to an eternity of torment in a lake of fire surrounded by demons. The wonder is not so much why more people did not call for reform as that anyone was brave enough to try.

The Protestant Reformation did not arise as an attempt to overthrow the power of the Church but began simply as yet another effort at reforming ecclesiastical abuse and corruption.

Martin Luther (1483-1546 AD) was a highly-educated German priest and monk who moved from concern to outrage over the abuses of the Church. He criticized the sale of indulgences as a money-making scheme having no biblical authority and no spiritual worth in his famous Ninety-Five Theses (1517 AD) and opposed the Church's teachings on a number of other matters.

Luther was condemned by Pope Leo X in 1520 AD who demanded he renounce his criticism or face excommunication. When Luther refused to recant, Pope Leo moved ahead with the excommunication in 1521 AD, and Luther became an outlaw. Like Wycliffe, Hus, and others before him, Luther was only stating the obvious in calling for an end to rampant abuse and corruption. Like Wycliffe, he translated the Bible from Latin into the vernacular (Wycliffe from Latin to Middle English and Luther from Latin to
German), opposed the concept of sacerdotalism whereby a priest is necessary as an intermediary between a believer and God, and maintained that the Bible and prayer were all one needed to communicate directly with God.

In making these claims, of course, he not only undermined the authority of the Pope but rendered that position as well as those of the cardinals, bishops, archbishops, priests, and others ineffectual and obsolete.

**MARTIN LUTHER**

According to Luther, salvation was granted by the grace of God, not by the good deeds of human beings, and so all of the works the Church required of people were of no eternal use and only served to fill the Church's treasury and build their grand cathedrals.

Owing to the political climate in Germany, and Luther's own charisma and intelligence, his effort at reform became the movement which would break the power of the Church. Other reformers such as Huldrych Zwingli (1484-1531 AD) and John Calvin (1509-1564 AD) broke new ground in their own regions and many others followed suit.

The monopoly the Church held on religious belief and practice was broken, and a new era of greater spiritual freedom was begun, but it was not without cost. In their zeal to throw off the oppression of the medieval Church, the newly liberated protestors destroyed monasteries, libraries, and cathedrals, the ruins of which still dot the European landscape in the present day.

## CONCLUSION

The Church had certainly become increasingly corrupt and oppressive and its clergy was frequently characterized far more by a love of worldly goods and pleasures than spiritual pursuits but, at the same time, the Church had initiated hospitals, colleges and universities, social systems for the care of the poor and the sick, and maintained religious orders which allowed women an outlet for their spirituality, imagination, and ambitions. These institutions became especially important during the Black Death pandemic of 1347-1352 AD which killed millions of people in Europe and significantly impacted people's faith in the vision of the Church.

The Protestant Reformation, unfortunately, destroyed much of the good the Church had done in reacting to the corruption it had fallen into and its perceived failure to meet the challenge of the plague outbreak. Eventually, the different movements would organize into the Christian Protestant sects recognizable today – Lutherans, Presbyterians, evangelicals, and so on – and set up their own institutes of higher learning, hospitals, and social programs. When the Reformation began, there was only the Church, the monolithic powerhouse of the middle Ages, which afterwards became only one option for religious expression among.

# END NOTES

*The church is historically unique. God entered into a particular covenant with this new people, through the saving work of his Son, and makes promises to them as revealed in Scripture. Church history is the story of how God has guarded, purified, chastised, and strengthened his undeserving people.*

*As visible outposts of the kingdom of Christ, churches are where one great story continually confronts and collides with the stories of this world and the present evil age. Church history tells the stories of that confrontation, in all of its beauty and messiness.*

*From the Scriptures we understand his ultimate purposes of redemption and his pledge to build his church. We are often without human explanation, however, for why his plans take a particular course.*

Made in United States
Orlando, FL
03 October 2023